Text © 2021 Zoë Tucker.
Illustrations © 2021 Salini Perera

First published in paperback in 2023 by
Wide Eyed Editions, an imprint of The Quarto Group.
100 Cummings Center, Suite 265D, Beverly, MA 01915, USA.
Tel: +1 978-282-9590 www.Quarto.com

A CIP record for this book is available from the
Library of Congress.

ISBN 978-0-7112-9027-3

The illustrations were created digitally
Set in Lelo

Published by Georgia Amson-Bradshaw
Designed by Zoë Tucker
Production by Dawn Cameron

Manufactured in Guangdong, China TT052023

9 8 7 6 5 4 3 2

FSC
www.fsc.org
MIX
Paper | Supporting
responsible forestry
FSC® C016973

written by
Zoë Tucker

illustrated by
Salini Perera

WE ARE THE
SUPREMES

WIDE EYED EDITIONS

Mary was excited!
Today was the high school
talent show and she
couldn't wait
to sing.

Talent Show

During her performance, she sang her heart out. Mary loved music, and being on stage was such a thrill!

Mary watched the other performers. Florence was up next. She had the sweetest voice Mary had ever heard.

After the show, Mary and Flo walked home together. They both lived on the east side of Detroit, in a big community called the Brewster-Douglass Housing Project.

The people who lived there were like one big family, and everyone looked after each other.

The girls' friendship grew as they spent all their time together singing along to records and practicing their dance moves.

ONE DAY, WE'LL BE THE BEST GIRL GROUP IN THE WORLD!

One day, Flo and Mary heard about an all-male group called The Primes who were looking for an all-girl group to sing with. They decided to audition!

AUDITIONS
3:00 PM
PRIMETTES
AT THE
CANDY SHOP

Another girl who lived across the street auditioned too. Her name was Diana.

Together they were
sensational!

They became The Primettes!
The newest girl-group on the block.

Being together was great fun and they each brought something special to the group.

Flo was strong and clever,

Mary was fun and bubbly,

and Diana was friendly and confident.

Soon The Primettes began performing at local parties and clubs.

Detroit was famous for its big car factories, not to mention its cool music scene. The girls always dressed to impress the movers and shakers of "Motor City!"

THE FILLMORE

**TONIGHT
THE PRIMES
WITH THE
THE PRIMETTES
7PM**

**TONIGHT
THE PRIMES
WITH THE
THE PRIMETTES
7PM**

TICKETS

Sometimes they sang
with a fourth singer. First a
girl called Betty, and then later, a girl
called Barbara, but Mary, Flo, and Diana
were the heart and soul of the group.

They rocked and bopped at "Sock Hops" all over town.

(A Sock Hop is just what it sounds like—a dance where people kicked off their shoes and danced and hopped around in their socks!)

The girls sounded so good,
a friend suggested they audition
for Motown Records, the most
famous record company in
the whole city.

At the time, Black musicians didn't have the same opportunities and rights as white musicians. It was very frustrating and unfair. But Motown Records was a Black-owned record company that was very successful. They were helping lots of Black musicians become pop stars. It was a big deal.

The manager of Motown was a man called Berry Gordy. He found the sharpest, coolest, funkiest artists in town. He was tough, but he knew his stuff. Mary, Flo, and Diana were desperate to be part of the scene.

At the audition, with hearts hammering, and butterflies in their stomachs, they sang their favorite song.

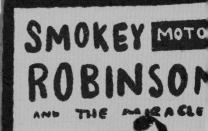

SMOKEY MOTO
ROBINSON
AND THE MIRACLE

They felt really sad and frustrated, but it made them even more determined to succeed!

For the next year the girls worked really hard.

They finished their schoolwork
AND practiced their music.

Mary taught them new
dance moves, and Flo made sure
they were all in perfect harmony.

Diana designed
and made all their
outfits,

and together they
became stronger, and
more polished than ever before.

Finally, their hard work paid off.
In 1961 Berry Gordy signed them to
Motown Records, but only on
one condition . . .

. . . That they choose a new name!

All the different
names were mixed up and
Flo was given the tricky task of picking.

She chose **"The Supremes."**

But Diana and Mary hated the new name,
and the three girls had a BIG fight!

Then they realized their shared dream was much more important than their silly squabble, and they quickly made up, as all good friends do.

Before long
The Supremes became
superstars.

They performed
all over America,

and their music was played
and loved all over the
world and beyond.

Their first
number one hit
"Where Did Our Love Go?"
was played to the crew of
Gemini 5 as they orbited the Earth!

The Supremes became much more than the best girl group in the world, they became a symbol of the changing times in America and people of all colors and nationalities idolized them.

It's amazing what you can do with your friends!

WE ARE THE SUPREMES

* Mary Wilson: March 6, 1944—February 8, 2021
* Florence Ballard: June 30, 1943—February 22, 1976
* Diana Ross: March 26, 1944

THE SUPREMES were the most successful female group of the 1960s. They had 12 number one hits, including five in a row which was a world record at the time. Three girls from downtown Detroit became a symbol of hope for a generation of young people who were growing up in the middle of the Civil Rights Movement of the 1950s and 60s, when Black people were fighting to be given the same rights as white people.

Berry Gordy founded Motown Records. He loved music and he believed it could unite people. From his home studio called Hitsville U.S.A he put together the best Black musicians and songwriters in the city to create amazing records. Everyone in Motown pitched in and worked as a team, each helping to make the best songs and performances they could. In the early days, Flo, Diana, and Mary sang with a fourth member, first Betty McGlown-Travis, then later Barbara Martin, though they both left before the Supremes became very famous. The girls also sang harmonies and did hand claps for other groups too. With a mix of pop, blues, gospel, and soul, the Motown artists created some seriously positive vibes!

At the time most television shows and radio stations didn't showcase Black artists, but Motown Records helped to change that. Their music topped the charts and they became known as the "Sound of Young America." Suddenly, The Supremes and fellow artists including Stevie Wonder, Marvin Gaye and Martha and the Vandellas were loved and idolized. They were booked for cool clubs and big TV shows and their songs were heard around the world. Motown Records became the most celebrated record company in history.

The Supremes didn't sing about politics—they sang about love—but Mary, Flo, and Diana used their fame to challenge the beliefs that white people held towards Black people by presenting a different image. Most of all they wanted to inspire and motivate the younger generation around them. They were always fun, professional, fashionable, and glamorous.

Times were tough, especially when they played to segregated audiences (where white and Black people were kept separate), but they worked very, very hard, and slowly over time their music united people and helped to break down racial barriers. Their friendship and determination paved the way for every girl band to have come along since. They worked against the odds and in doing so, offered hope to every little Black girl in the U.S.A.